Tigerology Trivia Challenge

Detroit Tigers Baseball

Tigerology
Trivia
Challenge

Detroit Tigers Baseball

Researched by Billy G. Wilcox III

Tom P. Rippey III & Paul F. Wilson, Editors

Kick The Ball, Ltd
Lewis Center, Ohio

Trivia by Kick The Ball, Ltd

College Football Trivia

Alabama Crimson Tide	Auburn Tigers	Boston College Eagles	Florida Gators
Georgia Bulldogs	LSU Tigers	Miami Hurricanes	Michigan Wolverines
Nebraska Cornhuskers	Notre Dame Fighting Irish	Ohio State Buckeyes	Oklahoma Sooners
Oregon Ducks	Penn State Nittany Lions	Southern Cal Trojans	Texas Longhorns

Pro Football Trivia

Arizona Cardinals	Buffalo Bills	Chicago Bears	Cleveland Browns
Denver Broncos	Green Bay Packers	Indianapolis Colts	Kansas City Chiefs
Minnesota Vikings	New England Patriots	Oakland Raiders	Pittsburgh Steelers
San Francisco 49ers	Washington Redskins		

Pro Baseball Trivia

Boston Red Sox	Chicago Cubs	Chicago White Sox	Cincinnati Reds
Detroit Tigers	Los Angeles Dodgers	New York Mets	New York Yankees
Philadelphia Phillies	Saint Louis Cardinals	San Francisco Giants	

College Basketball Trivia

Duke Blue Devils	Georgetown Hoyas	Indiana Hoosiers	Kansas Jayhawks
Kentucky Wildcats	Maryland Terrapins	Michigan State Spartans	North Carolina Tar Heels
Syracuse Orange	UConn Huskies	UCLA Bruins	

Pro Basketball Trivia

Boston Celtics	Chicago Bulls	Detroit Pistons	Los Angeles Lakers
Utah Jazz			

Visit **www.TriviaGameBooks.com** for more details.

This book is dedicated to our families and friends for your unwavering love, support, and your understanding of our pursuit of our passions. Thank you for everything you do for us and for making our lives complete.

Tigerology Trivia Challenge: Detroit Tigers Baseball;
First Edition 2010

Published by
Kick The Ball, Ltd
8595 Columbus Pike, Suite 197
Lewis Center, OH 43035
www.TriviaGameBooks.com

Designed, Formatted, and Edited by: Tom P. Rippey III & Paul F. Wilson
Researched by: Billy G. Wilcox III

For information on ordering this book in bulk at reduced prices, please email us at pfwilson@triviagamebooks.com.

International Standard Book Number: 978-1-934372-80-7

Printed and Bound in the United States of America

10 9 8 7 6 5 4 3 2 1

Table of Contents

Dear Friend,

Thank you for purchasing our *Tigerology Trivia Challenge* game book!

We have made every attempt to verify the accuracy of the questions and answers contained in this book. However it is still possible that from time to time an error has been made by us or our researchers. In the event you find a question or answer that is questionable or inaccurate, we ask for your understanding and thank you for bringing it to our attention so we may improve future editions of this book. Please email us at tprippey@triviagamebooks.com with those observations and comments.

Have fun playing *Tigerology Trivia Challenge*!

Tom and Paul

Tom Rippey and Paul Wilson
Co-Founders, Kick The Ball, Ltd

PS – You can discover more about all of our current trivia game books by visiting www.TriviaGameBooks.com.

Book Format:

There are four quarters, each made up of fifty questions. Each quarter's questions have assigned point values. Questions are designed to get progressively more difficult as you proceed through each quarter, as well as through the book itself. Most questions are in a four-option multiple-choice format so that you will at least have a 25% chance of getting a correct answer for some of the more challenging questions.

We have even added extra innings in the event of a tie, or just in case you want to keep playing a little longer.

Game Options:

One Player -
To play on your own, simply answer each of the questions in all the quarters, and in the overtime section, if you'd like. Use the Player / Team Score Sheet to record your answers and the quarter Answer Keys to check your answers. Calculate each quarter's points and the total for the game at the bottom of the Player / Team Score Sheet to determine your final score.

Two or More Players –
To play with multiple players decide if you will all be competing with each other individually, or if you will form and play as teams. Each player / team will then have its own Player / Team Score Sheet to record its answer. You can use the quarter Answer Keys to check your answers and to calculate your final scores.

The Player / Team Score Sheets have been designed so that each team can answer all questions or you can divide the questions up in any combination you would prefer. For example, you may want to alternate questions if two players are playing or answer every third question for three players, etc. In any case, simply record your response to your questions in the corresponding quarter and question number on the Player / Team Score Sheet.

A winner will be determined by multiplying the total number of correct answers for each quarter by the point value per quarter, then adding together the final total for all quarters combined. Play the game again and again by alternating the questions that your team is assigned so that you will answer a different set of questions each time you play.

You Create the Game -
There are countless other ways of using *Tigerology Trivia Challenge* questions. It is limited only to your imagination. Examples might be using them at your tailgate or other professional baseball related party. Players / Teams who answer questions incorrectly may have to perform a required action, or winners may receive special prizes. Let us know what other games you come up with!

Have fun!

1) What year did the Tigers join the American League?

Answers begin on page 17

    A) 1901
    B) 1907
    C) 1914
    D) 1920

2) What are the Tigers' official colors?

    A) Black and White
    B) Gray and Blue
    C) Navy Blue and Gray
    D) Navy Blue, White, and Orange

3) What is the name of the Tigers' current home stadium?

    A) Ford Field
    B) Memorial Stadium
    C) Comerica Park
    D) Tiger Stadium

4) What year did the Tigers acquire Ty Cobb?

    A) 1902
    B) 1905
    C) 1908
    D) 1911

5) Who was the Tigers' 2009 opening-day starting pitcher?

    A)   Dontrelle Willis
    B)   Jeremy Bonderman
    C)   Justin Verlander
    D)   Edwin Jackson

6) In which American League division do the Tigers play?

    A)   West
    B)   Central
    C)   North
    D)   East

7) When was the most recent season the Tigers won greater than 100 games?

    A)   1968
    B)   1984
    C)   1992
    D)   2006

8) Who has the longest tenure managing the Tigers?

    A)   Ty Cobb
    B)   Hughie Jennings
    C)   Sparky Anderson
    D)   Steve O'Neill

9) Where did Tigers great Kirk Gibson attend college?

- A) Notre Dame
- B) Syracuse
- C) Penn State
- D) Michigan State

10) What is the name of the Tigers' official mascot?

- A) Paws
- B) Tony
- C) Buster
- D) Striper

11) Who was the Tigers' opponent in their most recent World Series appearance?

- A) Chicago Cubs
- B) St. Louis Cardinals
- C) Cincinnati Reds
- D) San Diego Padres

12) The Tigers have won the American League Pennant greater than 15 times.

- A) True
- B) False

13) How many years did Detroit call Tiger Stadium home?

    A) 64
    B) 75
    C) 88
    D) 94

14) Which former Tiger was nicknamed "the Bird"?

    A) Mark Fidrych
    B) Chet Lemon
    C) Norm Cash
    D) Lance Parrish

15) Detroit's stadium has a seating capacity over 50,000.

    A) True
    B) False

16) Who is the Tigers' current manager?

    A) Alan Trammell
    B) Buddy Bell
    C) Jim Leyland
    D) Phil Garner

17) Who was the Tigers' opponent in the play-in game at the end of the 2009 regular season?

A) Chicago White Sox
B) Cleveland Indians
C) Kansas City Royals
D) Minnesota Twins

18) What year did the Tigers play in their first-ever World Series?

A) 1907
B) 1916
C) 1934
D) 1946

19) Who holds the Tigers' career record for games pitched?

A) Mickey Lolich
B) John Hiller
C) George Mullin
D) Todd Jones

20) Who hit the most home runs for the Tigers in 2009?

A) Curtis Granderson
B) Brandon Inge
C) Magglio Ordonez
D) Miguel Cabrera

21) What was the original name of Tiger Stadium?

   A) Ford Park
   B) Memorial Stadium
   C) Navin Field
   D) Detroit Municipal Stadium

22) What year did the Tigers win their first-ever World Series?

   A) 1921
   B) 1935
   C) 1953
   D) 1966

23) How many total runs did the Tigers score in the 2009 regular season?

   A) 743
   B) 779
   C) 801
   D) 828

24) Did the Tigers win greater than 90 games during the 2009 regular season?

   A) Yes
   B) No

25) Who was the last Tiger to win the American League Most Valuable Player Award?

    A) Alan Trammell
    B) Willie Hernandez
    C) Cecil Fielder
    D) Magglio Ordonez

26) How many times did Ty Cobb steal home during his Tiger career?

    A) 14
    B) 23
    C) 36
    D) 50

27) Who was the most recent Tiger to win a Cy Young Award?

    A) Jack Morris
    B) Bill Gullickson
    C) Willie Hernandez
    D) Justin Verlander

28) To what branch of the U.S. Armed Forces did the Tigers' Hank Greenberg belong?

    A) Army
    B) Navy
    C) Marines
    D) Coast Guard

29) Has a Tigers player ever hit four home runs in a single game?

    A) Yes
    B) No

30) Who was the first-ever player to have his jersey number retired by Detroit?

    A) Hank Greenberg
    B) Al Kaline
    C) Kirk Gibson
    D) Denny McLain

31) How many times has a Tigers pitcher won 20 or more games in a season?

    A) 29
    B) 36
    C) 44
    D) 50

32) How many times have the Tigers won 100 or more games in a season?

    A) 3
    B) 5
    C) 7
    D) 9

33) In which country was Tigers outfielder Magglio Ordonez born?

    A) Dominican Republic
    B) Mexico
    C) Canada
    D) Venezuela

34) What is the Tigers' team record for consecutive games with a home run?

    A) 13
    B) 19
    C) 25
    D) 31

35) Did the Tigers have a winning record at the All-Star break in 2009?

    A) Yes
    B) No

36) Which Tigers pitcher had the most wins in 2009?

    A) Edwin Jackson
    B) Rick Porcello
    C) Zach Miner
    D) Justin Verlander

37) Who is the only Tigers player to record five stolen bases in the same game?

    A) Johnny Neun
    B) Ron LeFlore
    C) Lou Whitaker
    D) Ty Cobb

38) Against which American League team did the Tigers have the highest winning percentage during the 2009 regular season?

    A) Kansas City Royals
    B) New York Yankees
    C) Chicago White Sox
    D) Cleveland Indians

39) How many all-time World Series have the Tigers won?

    A) 2
    B) 4
    C) 5
    D) 7

40) What was Cecil Fielder's nickname while playing for the Tigers?

    A) Big Daddy
    B) Moose
    C) Chief
    D) The Hammer

41) Who is the only Tiger to have 100 or more RBIs during the 2009 season?

    A)   Magglio Ordonez
    B)   Brandon Inge
    C)   Miguel Cabrera
    D)   Placido Polanco

42) How many times have the Tigers scored greater than 800 runs in a season?

    A)   11
    B)   16
    C)   21
    D)   26

43) No Detroit Tigers pitcher has thrown a perfect game.

    A)   True
    B)   False

44) How many Tigers were selected to the 2009 All-Star team?

    A)   2
    B)   3
    C)   4
    D)   5

45) Who is the only Tigers player to hit two grand slams in a single game?

    A) Al Kaline
    B) Tony Clark
    C) Cecil Fielder
    D) Jim Northrup

46) What were the most Tigers players selected as All-Stars in a single season?

    A) 4
    B) 6
    C) 8
    D) 10

47) How many Tigers managers lasted one season or less?

    A) 8
    B) 10
    C) 12
    D) 14

48) Who is the only Tigers pitcher to get a base hit 2009?

    A) Justin Verlander
    B) Alfredo Figaro
    C) Jeremy Bonderman
    D) Rick Porcello

49) What is the nickname of the AAA team affiliated with the Detroit Tigers?

    A) Toledo Mud Hens
    B) West Michigan Whitecaps
    C) Oneonta Tigers
    D) Erie SeaWolves

50) Who was the most recent Tiger to be named American League Rookie of the Year?

    A) Lou Whitaker
    B) Justin Verlander
    C) Travis Fryman
    D) Armando Galarraga

On May 15, 1976, with their scheduled starting pitcher out with the flu, the Tigers turned to rookie Mark "The Bird" Fidrych. Fidrych threw a two-hit complete game defeating the Indians 2-1. The 6'3" right-hander dazzled fans with his 93 mph fastball and his on-field antics, which included: getting on his knees and manicuring the mound, talking to himself, talking to the baseball, and demonstratively circling the mound after every out. He then lost his next start at Boston, but followed with two consecutive 11-inning victories. "Bird-Mania" was alive and attendance figures were showing it. "Bird Watchers" packed Tiger Stadium to watch Fidrych mow through American League hitters, putting on a side-show along the way. In Fidrych's starts, the Tigers averaged 18,000 more fans than other games with attendance rising more than 400,000 over the course of the season. Fidrych finished the season with a 19-9 record, led the majors with a 2.34 ERA, and won the AL Rookie of the Year award. An injury the next season led to his early retirement from baseball. Fidrych tragically passed away in 2009, but Tigers fans will always remember 1976 as "The Year of the Bird".

Tigerology Trivia Challenge

1) A – 1901 (Detroit was one of eight charter members of the American League, which formed in 1901.)

2) D – Navy Blue, White, and Orange (The orange only appears on the Tigers' away uniforms. They are the only team in MLB to have a color appear on their away uniforms that is not on their home uniforms.)

3) C – Comerica Park (The Tigers have played here since 2000. Stadium construction costs totaled $300 million.)

4) B – 1905 (Cobb played for the Tigers from 1905-26.)

5) C – Justin Verlander (Verlander got the 2009 opening day start for the Tigers at Toronto. The Tigers lost the game 5-12.)

6) B – Central (Other teams in the division include the Chicago White Sox, Cleveland Indians, Kansas City Royals, and Minnesota Twins.)

7) B – 1984 (The Tigers were 104-58 in 1984, winning the AL East by 15 games over the Toronto Blue Jays.)

8) C – Sparky Anderson (Anderson managed the Tigers for 17 seasons from 1979-95.)

9) D – Michigan State (Gibson played just one year of college baseball, hitting .390 with 16 home runs, 52 RBIs, and 21 stolen bases.)

10) A – Paws (Paws made his debut as the official Tigers mascot in 1995.)

11) B – St. Louis Cardinals (The Tigers were defeated in the 2006 World Series by the Cardinals in five games.)

12) B – False (The Tigers won the AL Pennant 10 times.)

13) C – 88 (Tiger Stadium was the home ballpark for the Tigers from 1912-99.)

14) A – Mark Fidrych (While pitching in the minors, Fidrych was given the nickname because of his resemblance to Big Bird from Sesame Street.)

15) B – False (Comerica Park has an official seating capacity of 41,782.)

16) C – Jim Leyland (Leyland has been the Tigers manager since 2006.)

17) D – Minnesota Twins (The Tigers and Twins ended the regular season tied atop the AL Central, forcing a play-in game. The Twins won the game 6-5 in 12 innings.)

18) A – 1907 (The Tigers lost the series 0-4 to the Chicago Cubs.)

19) B – John Hiller (Hiller appeared in 545 games as a Tiger from 1965-70 and 1972-80.)

20) D – Miguel Cabrera (Cabrera led Detroit with 34 home runs in 2009.)

21) C – Navin Field (Tiger Stadium was originally named Navin Field after Tigers owner Frank Navin.)

22) B – 1935 (The Tigers won their first World Series by defeating the Chicago Cubs four games to two in 1935.)

23) A – 743 (Detroit scored 743 runs during the 2009 season.)

24) B – No (The Tigers finished the 2009 season with an 86-77 record, a .528 winning percentage.)

25) B – Willie Hernandez (Hernandez won the AL MVP Award in 1984 after posting a 9-2 record with 32 saves.)

26) D – 50 (Cobb stole home 50 times in his Tiger career [1905-26].)

27) C – Willie Hernandez (Hernandez won the Cy Young Award in 1984 after recording 32 saves with a 1.92 ERA.)

28) A – Army (Greenberg's career was interrupted by a four-year stint in the Army during World War II.)

29) B – No (Detroit has never had a player hit four home runs in a game. The Tigers had a player hit three home runs in a game 19 times, most recently Carlos Pena at Cleveland in 2003.)

30) B – Al Kaline (Kaline's jersey number 6 was retired by the Tigers in 1980.)

31) C – 44 (The last Tiger to win 20 or more games in a season was Bill Gullickson [20-9] in 1991.)

32) B – 5 (The Tigers won 100 or more games in a season five times, most recently in 1984 when they posted a 104-58 record.)

33) D – Venezuela (Ordonez was born in Caracas, Venezuela on Jan. 28, 1974.)

34) C – 25 (The Tigers hit at least one home run in 25 consecutive games during the 1994 season.)

35) A – Yes (The Tigers were 48-39 at the All-Star break in 2009.)

36) D – Justin Verlander (Verlander finished the 2009 season with a 19-9 record.)

37) A – Johnny Neun (Neun stole five bases in a game versus Washington in 1927.)

38) D – Cleveland Indians (The Tigers were 14-4 versus the Indians in 2009, a .778 winning percentage.)

39) B – 4 (1935, 1945, 1968, and 1984)

40) A – Big Daddy (Fielder earned the nickname "Big Daddy" while playing for the Tigers [1990-96].)

41) C – Miguel Cabrera (Cabrera led the Tigers with 103 RBIs in 2009.)

42) D – 26 (The Tigers have scored 800+ runs in a season 26 times, most recently in 2008 when they scored 821 runs.)

43) A – True (The Tigers have never had a pitcher throw a perfect game.)

44) C – 4 (Pitchers Justin Verlander and Edwin Jackson, third baseman Brandon Inge, and outfielder Curtis Granderson)

45) D – Jim Northrup (Northrup hit two grand slams in a game at Cleveland in 1968.)

46) B – 6 (The Tigers had six players elected to the All-Star Game in both 1985 and 1986.)

47) B – 10 (Gene Stallings [1901], Frank Dwyer [1902], Bobby Lowe [1904], Billy Hitchcock [1960], Joe Gordon [1960], Frank Skaff [1966], Joe Schultz [1973], Les Moss [1979], Dick Tracewski [1979], and Luis Pujols [2002])

48) D – Rick Porcello (Porcello recorded two hits in five at-bats for the Tigers in 2009, the only pitcher on the staff to get a hit.)

49) A – Toledo Mud Hens (The Toledo Mud Hens of the International League have been the AAA affiliate of the Tigers since 1987.)

50) B – Justin Verlander (He won the award in 2006 with a 17-9 record and 3.63 ERA.)

Note: All answers valid as of the end of the 2009 season, unless otherwise indicated in the question itself.

1) What year did "Tigers" appear on Detroit's home uniforms?

Answers begin on page 37

   A) 1949
   B) 1960
   C) 1972
   D) 1986

2) What number did Tigers great Hank Greenberg wear?

   A) #5
   B) #9
   C) #14
   D) #23

3) Not including 2010 inductees, how many players have been inducted into the National Baseball Hall of Fame with the Tigers as their primary team?

   A) 11
   B) 13
   C) 15
   D) 17

4) Where did the Tigers play their home games before Tiger Stadium was built?

   A) Briggs Stadium
   B) University of Detroit
   C) Bennett Park
   D) Polo Grounds

5) Did the Tigers have a winning record on the road during the regular season in 2009?

    A) Yes
    B) No

6) How many times did Detroit sweep a series during the 2009 regular season?

    A) 3
    B) 5
    C) 7
    D) 9

7) When was the first time a Tiger hit 40 or more home runs in a single season?

    A) 1914
    B) 1925
    C) 1937
    D) 1948

8) Which of the following Tigers players won two consecutive American League Most Valuable Player Awards?

    A) Mickey Cochrane
    B) Charlie Gehringer
    C) Hank Greenberg
    D) Hal Newhouser

9) The Tigers had a winning record in one-run games during the 2009 season.

    A) True
    B) False

10) Which American League opponent have the Tigers played the fewest times during the regular season?

    A) Texas Rangers
    B) Seattle Mariners
    C) Tampa Bay Rays
    D) Boston Red Sox

11) What is the Tigers' all-time winning percentage against the White Sox?

    A) .485
    B) .503
    C) .529
    D) .618

12) Who is the most recent Tigers pitcher to lead the American League in strikeouts?

    A) Jeremy Bonderman
    B) Jack Morris
    C) Mark Fidrych
    D) Justin Verlander

13) How many times have Tigers pitchers been awarded the Cy Young Award?

    A) 1
    B) 3
    C) 5
    D) 7

14) When did the Tigers first record a winning season in the American League?

    A) 1901
    B) 1904
    C) 1907
    D) 1910

15) What is the Tigers' record for most hits as a team in a single season?

    A) 1,579
    B) 1,688
    C) 1,724
    D) 1,853

16) Has any Tigers player ever hit greater than four grand slams in a single season?

    A) Yes
    B) No

17) What is the Tigers' record for fewest errors as a team during the regular season?

A) 67
B) 76
C) 88
D) 99

18) Which Tigers pitcher had the lowest ERA in 2009 (minimum 50 appearances)?

A) Edwin Jackson
B) Ryan Perry
C) Brandon Lyon
D) Fernando Rodney

19) How many times has a Tigers player been walked 125 or more times in a single season?

A) 0
B) 2
C) 4
D) 6

20) The Tigers have won greater than 10,000 all-time regular-season games since joining the American League.

A) True
B) False

21) Which team have the Tigers played the most (number of series played) in the World Series?

    A) Cincinnati Reds
    B) St. Louis Cardinals
    C) Chicago Cubs
    D) Pittsburgh Pirates

22) Which Tigers player hit the first home run at Comerica Park?

    A) Gregg Jefferies
    B) Dean Palmer
    C) Bobby Higginson
    D) Juan Gonzalez

23) Who holds the Tigers' record for highest batting average by a rookie?

    A) Lu Blue
    B) Hank Greenberg
    C) Dale Alexander
    D) Roy Johnson

24) Who was the Tigers' most recent Gold Glove winner?

    A) Placido Polanco
    B) Ivan Rodriguez
    C) Gary Pettis
    D) Carlos Guillen

25) Which pitcher is Detroit's all-time saves leader?

    A) Aurelio Lopez
    B) Mike Henneman
    C) Guillermo Hernandez
    D) Todd Jones

26) Who is the Tigers' current pitching coach?

    A) Chuck Hernandez
    B) Jeff Jones
    C) Rick Knapp
    D) Scott Pickens

27) The Tigers had a winning record in inter-league play in 2009.

    A) True
    B) False

28) In their history, how many times has Detroit turned a triple-play?

    A) 15
    B) 21
    C) 27
    D) 33

29) How many games did the Tigers spend in first place during the 2009 season?

  A) 79
  B) 98
  C) 123
  D) 146

30) What is Detroit's all-time winning percentage in home openers?

  A) .497
  B) .520
  C) .537
  D) .578

31) Has any Tiger ever won the All-Star Game MVP Award?

  A) Yes
  B) No

32) Against which American League team do the Tigers have their highest all-time winning percentage (min. 300 games played)?

  A) Cleveland Indians
  B) Kansas City Royals
  C) Texas Rangers
  D) Seattle Mariners

33) Who is the only Tigers pitcher to record 16 strikeouts in a single game?

    A) Tommy Bridges
    B) Denny McLain
    C) Mickey Lolich
    D) Jack Morris

34) Which season did the Tigers first face the Yankees in the postseason?

    A) 1973
    B) 1984
    C) 1997
    D) 2006

35) What is the Tigers' record for most runs allowed in a single game?

    A) 22
    B) 24
    C) 26
    D) 28

36) Who is Detroit's career RBI leader?

    A) Ty Cobb
    B) Al Kaline
    C) Hank Greenberg
    D) Sam Crawford

37) Who was Detroit's first-ever opponent in Comerica Park?

    A)   Tampa Bay Rays
    B)   Seattle Mariners
    C)   Cleveland Indians
    D)   Kansas City Royals

38) How many times has a Tiger hit for the cycle (single, double, triple, and home run in the same game)?

    A)   4
    B)   6
    C)   8
    D)   10

39) Which Tigers pitcher holds the team record for lowest ERA in a season?

    A)   Hal Newhouser
    B)   Mark Fidrych
    C)   Ed Summers
    D)   Denny McLain

40) Ty Cobb is the only Tiger to hit over .400 in a season.

    A)   True
    B)   False

41) Who holds the Tigers' record for stolen bases in a season?

    A) Ron LeFlore
    B) Brian Hunter
    C) Tony Phillips
    D) Ty Cobb

42) How many players have played over 2,000 games as a Tiger?

    A) 3
    B) 5
    C) 7
    D) 9

43) What is the nickname of the AA team affiliated with the Detroit Tigers?

    A) GCL Tigers
    B) Lakeland Flying Tigers
    C) Erie SeaWolves
    D) West Michigan Whitecaps

44) How many times have the Tigers been swept in the World Series?

    A) 1
    B) 2
    C) 3
    D) 4

45) Which Tiger had his jersey number retired, but is not a member of the National Baseball Hall of Fame?

    A) Charlie Gehringer
    B) Hal Newhouser
    C) Al Kaline
    D) Willie Horton

46) When did the Tigers last host the All-Star Game?

    A) 1999
    B) 2002
    C) 2005
    D) 2008

47) How many players have had their jersey number retired by the Tigers?

    A) 3
    B) 5
    C) 7
    D) 9

48) How many times did Sparky Anderson win American League Manager of the Year as a Tiger?

    A) 1
    B) 2
    C) 3
    D) 4

49) What decade did the Tigers have the highest regular-season winning percentage?

    A) 1920s
    B) 1940s
    C) 1960s
    D) 1980s

50) Who was the last Detroit pitcher to start an All-Star Game?

    A) Jack Morris
    B) David Wells
    C) Justin Verlander
    D) Kenny Rogers

Before becoming the Tiger's first-round draft pick (12th overall) in 1978, Kirk Gibson was a two-sport star at Michigan State University. Gibson, a 6'3" wide receiver, went to East Lansing on a football scholarship, putting up huge numbers. He finished his football career with 112 receptions for 2,347 yards and 24 touchdowns, all Spartan records at the time. Gibson was named First Team All-American in 1978, and at 227 pounds was clocked by NFL scouts at 4.2 in the 40-yard dash. He was drafted by the St. Louis Cardinals in the 7th round of the 1979 NFL Draft, but decided to stick with baseball. Good choice.

1) B – 1960 (The word "Tigers" appeared on Detroit's home uniforms for the first and only time during the 1960 season.)

2) A – #5 (Greenberg wore #5 for the Tigers from 1930-46.)

3) A – 11 (The most recent Tiger inductee was Hal Newhouser in 1992.)

4) C – Bennett Park (The Tigers played at Bennett Park from 1901-11. Bennett Park was torn down and Tiger Stadium was built on the same grounds.)

5) B – No (The Tigers were 35-47 on the road in 2009, for a .427 winning percentage.)

6) D – 9 (The Tigers swept a three-game series versus the Indians three times, against the Rangers twice, and against the A's, Brewers, Cubs, and Rays once each.)

7) C – 1937 (Hank Greenberg hit 40 home runs for the Tigers in 1937.)

8) D – Hal Newhouser (Newhouser won the AL MVP Award in 1944 and 1945.)

9) A – True (The Tigers posted a 28-22 record in games decided by one run.)

10) C – Tampa Bay Rays (The Tigers have played the Rays a total of 89 times [45-44]. The Rays franchise was established in 1998.)

11) B – .503 (The Tigers are 999-988-15 all-time versus the Chicago White Sox, for a .503 winning percentage.)

12) D – Justin Verlander (Verlander led the AL with 269 strikeouts in 2009.)

13) B – 3 (Denny McLain [1968 and 1969] and Willie
    Hernandez [1984])

14) A – 1901 (Detroit posted a 74-61 record in their
    inaugural season of 1901.)

15) C– 1,724 (The Tigers had 1,724 hits in 5,461 at-bats
    during the 1921 season, for a .316 team batting
    average.)

16) B – No (Rudy York [1938] and Jim Northrup [1968]
    each hit four grand slams in a season, but no Tiger
    has ever hit five.)

17) A – 67 (The Tigers committed just 67 errors during the
    strike-shortened 1981 season.)

18) C – Brandon Lyon (Lyon posted a 2.86 ERA in 65
    appearances for the Tigers in 2009.)

19) C – 4 (Eddie Yost [135 times in 1959 and 125 times in
    1960], Roy Cullenbine [137 times in 1947], and
    Tony Phillips [132 times in 1993])

20) B – False (The Tigers have won 8,564 all-time games.)

21) C – Chicago Cubs (The Tigers have faced the Cubs
    four times in the World Series [1907, 1908, 1935,
    and 1945]. The Tigers won twice.)

22) D – Juan Gonzalez (Gonzalez hit the historic home run
    off of Tampa Bay's Ryan Rupe in 2000.)

23) C – Dale Alexander (Alexander hit .343 for Detroit in
    1929.)

24) A – Placido Polanco (The second baseman won his
    second Gold Glove Award in 2009 after committing
    just two errors.)

25) D – Todd Jones (Jones recorded 235 career saves with the Tigers [1997-2001, 2006-08].)

26) C – Rick Knapp (Knapp has been Detroit's pitching coach since 2008.)

27) A – True (The Tigers were 10-8 [.556] versus the National League in 2009.)

28) D– 33 (The Tigers have turned 33 triple-plays in their history. The most recent one came in 2001 versus Seattle.)

29) D – 146 (The Tigers led the AL Central for 146 games before becoming the first team in MLB history to blow a three-game lead with just four games left to play.)

30) C – .537 (The Tigers are 58-50-1 [.537] all-time in home openers.)

31) B – No (The Tigers have never had a player win the All-Star Game MVP Award.)

32) D – Seattle Mariners (The Tigers are 190-156-1 all-time versus the Mariners, for a .549 winning percentage.)

33) C – Mickey Lolich (Lolich fanned 16 batters in a game twice during the 1969 season [vs. California and vs. Seattle].)

34) D – 2006 (The Tigers defeated the Yankees three games to one in the 2006 ALDS.)

35) C – 26 (The Tigers lost 5-26 to the Kansas City Royals in 2004.)

36) A – Ty Cobb (Cobb had 1,828 RBIs for the Tigers from 1905-26.)

37) B – Seattle Mariners (The Tigers beat the Mariners 5-2 in 2000. Brian Moehler was the winning pitcher for Detroit.)

38) D – 10 (Detroit had a player hit for the cycle 10 times, most recently Carlos Guillen at Tampa Bay in 2006.)

39) C – Ed Summers (Summers set the record in 1908 with a 1.64 ERA.)

40) B – False (Harry Heilmann hit .403 for Detroit in 1923. Cobb had a batting average of .420 in 1911, .409 in 1912, and .401 in 1922.)

41) D – Ty Cobb (Cobb stole 96 bases for the Tigers in 1915.)

42) A – 7 (Al Kaline [2,834], Ty Cobb [2,805], Lou Whitaker [2,390], Charlie Gehringer [2,323], Alan Trammell [2,293], Sam Crawford [2,114], and Norm Cash [2,018])

43) C – Erie SeaWolves (The Erie SeaWolves of the Eastern League have been the Tigers' AA affiliate since 2001.)

44) B – 1 (The Tigers were swept by the Cubs in 1907.)

45) D – Willie Horton (Horton's #23 was retired by the Tigers in 2000.)

46) C – 2005 (Comerica Park hosted the 2005 All-Star Game, a 7-5 AL victory. Baltimore's Miguel Tejada was named MVP.)

47) B – 5 (Charlie Gehringer [#2], Hank Greenberg [#5], Al Kaline [#6], Hal Newhouser [#16], and Willie Horton [#23])

48) B – 2 (Anderson won the award in 1984 and 1987.)

49) C – 1960s (The Tigers were 882-729 during the 1960s, for a .547 winning percentage.)

50) D – Kenny Rogers (Rogers started the 2006 All-Star Game.)

Note: All answers valid as of the end of the 2009 season, unless otherwise indicated in the question itself.

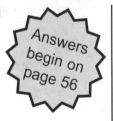

Answers begin on page 56

1) What is the Tiger's career record for grand slams hit by a single player?

 A) 6
 B) 8
 C) 10
 D) 12

2) How did the Tigers' Schoolboy Rowe get his nickname?

 A) Was Also a School Teacher
 B) Played on a Men's Team While in High School
 C) Never Finished High School
 D) His Baby-Face

3) When was the most recent season the Tigers failed to go .500?

 A) 1994
 B) 1999
 C) 2004
 D) 2008

4) Which Tigers manager has the most career wins?

 A) Hughie Jennings
 B) Bucky Harris
 C) Sparky Anderson
 D) Ralph Houk

5) Virgil Trucks is the only Tiger to throw greater than one no-hitter.

    A)   True
    B)   False

6) Which of the following positions is not represented by a Tiger in the National Baseball Hall of Fame?

    A)   Catcher
    B)   Left Field
    C)   Relief Pitcher
    D)   Second Base

7) Who has the highest career winning percentage of a Tigers pitcher with at least 100 career wins?

    A)   Bill Donovan
    B)   George Mullin
    C)   Jack Morris
    D)   Denny McLain

8) How many different pitchers did the Tigers use during the 2009 regular season?

    A)   18
    B)   21
    C)   24
    D)   27

9) What is the Tigers' all-time winning percentage against the Minnesota Twins?

   A) .441
   B) .489
   C) .518
   D) .556

10) Has Detroit retired Sparky Anderson's jersey number?

   A) Yes
   B) No

11) Who holds the Tigers' career record for home runs?

   A) Norm Cash
   B) Cecil Fielder
   C) Willie Horton
   D) Al Kaline

12) Which Tigers pitcher won the most career postseason games?

   A) Denny McLain
   B) Jack Morris
   C) Tommy Bridges
   D) George Mullin

13) What are the most errors the Tigers have committed in a single season?

    A) 318
    B) 355
    C) 381
    D) 410

14) Which Tigers catcher did not win a Gold Glove Award for Detroit?

    A) Bill Freehan
    B) Brad Ausmus
    C) Lance Parrish
    D) Ivan Rodriguez

15) Which Tigers manager had the highest winning percentage (minimum 3 seasons)?

    A) Mickey Cochrane
    B) Hughie Jennings
    C) Buddy Bell
    D) Sparky Anderson

16) How many Tigers players have recorded 250 or more stolen bases?

    A) 2
    B) 4
    C) 6
    D) 8

17) Who was the most recent Tigers player to be named the American League Home Run Champion?

    A) Cecil Fielder
    B) Dean Palmer
    C) Miguel Cabrera
    D) Magglio Ordonez

18) Detroit led the American League in fielding percentage in 2009.

    A) True
    B) False

19) When was the most recent season the leading player for the Tigers had fewer than 75 RBIs?

    A) 1988
    B) 1993
    C) 1998
    D) 2003

20) What is the current marked distance to the center field wall at Comerica Park?

    A) 390'
    B) 400'
    C) 410'
    D) 420'

21) Who was the most recent Tiger to lead the team in batting average, home runs, and RBIs in the same season?

    A) Tony Clark
    B) Randall Simon
    C) Magglio Ordonez
    D) Dmitri Young

22) Who was the last Tiger to wear the jersey number 42?

    A) Phil Nevin
    B) Fernando Hernandez
    C) Omar Olivares
    D) Matt Walbeck

23) Lou Whitaker played more career games at second base than any other Tiger.

    A) True
    B) False

24) When was the most recent season the Tigers, as a team, had a batting average of .275 or higher?

    A) 1998
    B) 2001
    C) 2004
    D) 2007

25) Did Ty Cobb play his entire career with the Tigers?

    A) Yes
    B) No

26) Which Tiger played in the most games during the 2009 regular season?

    A) Placido Polanco
    B) Curtis Granderson
    C) Aubrey Huff
    D) Brandon Inge

27) Which Tiger hit a club record five home runs in the 2006 postseason?

    A) Sean Casey
    B) Curtis Granderson
    C) Craig Monroe
    D) Magglio Ordonez

28) Who did the Tigers play in their 2009 home opener?

    A) Los Angeles Angels of Anaheim
    B) Texas Rangers
    C) Chicago White Sox
    D) Tampa Bay Rays

29) Todd Jones is the only Tigers pitcher with150 or more career saves.

    A) True
    B) False

30) What is the combined winning percentage of Tigers mangers who lasted one season or less?

    A) .401
    B) .445
    C) .518
    D) .564

31) Which legendary rock band opened their 1996 reunion tour at Detroit's Tiger Stadium?

    A) The Eagles
    B) Black Sabbath
    C) KISS
    D) Fleetwood Mac

32) What are the most consecutive losses the Tigers have ever had in one season?

    A) 10
    B) 13
    C) 16
    D) 19

33) What is the Tigers' team record for stolen bases in a season?

   A) 203
   B) 222
   C) 258
   D) 280

34) What are the fewest losses by the Tigers in one season?

   A) 45
   B) 49
   C) 53
   D) 57

35) Did any Tiger have greater than 250 assists during the 2009 regular season?

   A) Yes
   B) No

36) Which player holds the Tigers' record for most at-bats in a single season?

   A) Curtis Granderson
   B) Tony Phillips
   C) Ty Cobb
   D) Harvey Kuenn

37) Who was Detroit's first-round draft pick in 2009?

    A) Edwin Gomez
    B) Jacob Turner
    C) Michael Rockett
    D) Wade Gaynor

38) Who holds the Tigers' record for runs scored in a career?

    A) Ty Cobb
    B) Al Kaline
    C) Lou Whitaker
    D) Charlie Gehringer

39) Who is the last Tigers pitcher to hit a home run?

    A) Dontrelle Willis
    B) Kenny Rogers
    C) Jason Johnson
    D) Hideo Nomo

40) When was the most recent season the leading hitter for the Tigers had a batting average below .300?

    A) 1999
    B) 2001
    C) 2005
    D) 2008

41) Who is the only Tigers pitcher to win the American League Triple Crown (Wins, ERA, Strikeouts)?

    A) Denny McLain
    B) Hal Newhouser
    C) Jack Morris
    D) Dizzy Trout

42) What is the Tigers' record for most innings played in a single game?

    A) 18
    B) 20
    C) 22
    D) 24

43) Did the Tigers' manager Jim Leyland ever play in the Major Leagues?

    A) Yes
    B) No

44) Who was the most recent Tiger to hit an inside-the-park home run?

    A) Edgar Renteria
    B) Luis Polonia
    C) Curtis Granderson
    D) Robert Fick

45) How many Tigers players have a career on-base percentage of .400 or higher?

  A) 4
  B) 6
  C) 8
  D) 10

46) What color are the letters over the scoreboard at Comerica Park that spell "Tigers"?

  A) White
  B) Blue
  C) Orange
  D) Black

47) Who is the manager of the Toledo Mud Hens (AAA)?

  A) Bruce Fields
  B) Larry Parrish
  C) Alan Trammell
  D) Joe Sparks

48) How many Tigers have won the Roberto Clemente Award?

  A) 1
  B) 2
  C) 3
  D) 4

49) The Tigers had a higher batting average against right-handed pitchers than left-handed pitchers in 2009.

   A) True
   B) False

50) Which Tiger holds the club's career record for most times hit by pitch?

   A) Alan Trammell
   B) Ty Cobb
   C) Damion Easley
   D) Bill Freehan

Historic Tiger Stadium underwent many renovations and expansions throughout the years, but one of the most intriguing transformations came after the Tigers had already moved out. In 2000, with the Tigers playing at Comerica Park, Billy Crystal and a group of filmmakers chose Tiger Stadium to serve as the setting for the HBO movie 61*. 61* is the story of the Yankees' Roger Maris and Mickey Mantle during the 1961 season and their pursuit of the single-season home run record held by Babe Ruth. Yankee Stadium could not be used because it had undergone several changes since 1961 and no longer resembled the Yankee Stadium of the 1960s. Crystal chose Tiger Stadium because of the historic look and feel of old-time baseball. Though it had the feel of Yankee Stadium of the 1960s, the crew had to make some changes to convince fans that they were actually seeing Yankee Stadium. The right field fence was shortened and the seats were painted green. Also, a third deck and Bronx skyline were added after filming with the use of computer graphics. After filming ended, Tiger Stadium was returned to its previous form and the green paint was removed from the seats at a cost of $80,000. Tiger Stadium was credited at the end of the movie as playing the part of Yankee Stadium.

1) C – 10 (This record is shared by three Tigers: Rudy York [1934-45], Hank Greenberg [1930-46], and Cecil Fielder [1990-96].)

2) B – Played on a Men's Team While in High School (Lynwood Rowe pitched for a men's baseball team as a 15-year-old high school student.)

3) D – 2008 (Detroit finished the 2008 season with a 74-88 record, for a .457 winning percentage.)

4) C – Sparky Anderson (Anderson led the Tigers to 1,331 wins from 1979-95.)

5) A – True (Trucks threw no-hitters versus the Washington Senators and the New York Yankees, both during the 1952 season.)

6) C – Relief Pitcher (The Tigers are represented in Cooperstown by at least one player at every other position.)

7) D – Denny McLain (McLain was 117-62 for the Tigers from 1963-70, for a .654 winning percentage.)

8) B – 21 (The Tigers used 21 pitchers during the 2009 season, nine of whom pitched 50 or more innings.)

9) C – .518 (The Tigers are 1,032-958-17 all-time versus the Twins, for a .518 winning percentage.)

10) B – No (Though Anderson's #11 has not been re-issued since his 1995 retirement, it has not been officially retired by the Tigers.)

11) D – Al Kaline (Kaline hit 399 home runs for the Tigers from 1953-74.)

12) C – Tommy Bridges (Bridges won four postseason games for the Tigers [1934-35, 1940, and 1945].)

13) D – 410 (The Tigers committed 410 errors during the 1901 season.)

14) B – Brad Ausmus (Freehan won four Gold Glove Awards [1965-69], Parrish won three [1983-85], and Rodriguez also won three [2004 and 2006-07].)

15) A – Mickey Cochrane (Cochrane posted a 413-297 record [.582] managing the Tigers from 1934-38.)

16) B – 4 (Ty Cobb [865], Donie Bush [400], Sam Crawford [317], and Ron LeFlore [294])

17) C – Miguel Cabrera (Cabrera led the AL with 37 home runs in 2008.)

18) B – False (Detroit finished the season with a .985 fielding percentage. Toronto led the AL with a .988 fielding percentage.)

19) A – 1988 (Alan Trammell led the Tigers with 69 RBIs during the 1988 season.)

20) D – 420' (Comerica Park's dimensions are 345' down the LF line, 420' to center field, and 330' down the RF line.)

21) C – Magglio Ordonez (In 2007, Ordonez led the Tigers in batting average [.368], home runs [28], and RBIs [139].)

22) B – Fernando Hernandez (Hernandez wore #42 for two games with the Tigers in 1997. The #42 was retired by all of MLB in honor of Jackie Robinson that year.)

23) A – True (Whitaker played 2,308 career games at second base for the Tigers, 99 more than Charlie Gehringer.)

24) D – 2007 (The Tigers had a team-batting average of .287.)

25) B – No (Cobb played for the Tigers from 1905-26 before finishing his career with the Philadelphia Athletics [1927-28].)

26) D – Brandon Inge (Inge played in 161 of the Tigers 163 games in 2009.)

27) C – Craig Monroe (Monroe hit five home runs in the 2006 postseason, tying him for the career lead in postseason home runs with Hank Greenberg.)

28) B – Texas Rangers (The Tigers defeated the Rangers 15-2.)

29) B – False (Mike Henneman [1987-95] is second on the Tigers all-time saves list with 154 saves.)

30) B – .445 (Tigers managers who lasted one season or less had a combined record of 316-394.)

31) C – KISS (For the first time since 1979, the original members of KISS, in full make-up and costumes, performed together in 1996.)

32) D – 19 (The Tigers lost 19 consecutive games during the 1975 season.)

33) D – 280 (The Tigers stole a team-record 280 bases during the 1909 season.)

34) C – 53 (The Tigers were 101-53 in 1934.)

35) A – Yes (Placido Polanco [439], Adam Everett [282], and Brandon Inge [281])

36) D – Harvey Kuenn (Kuenn had 679 at-bats in 1953.)

37) B – Jacob Turner (Detroit drafted Turner, a RHP from Westminster Christian Academy in St. Louis, with the 9th overall pick.)

38) A – Ty Cobb (Cobb scored 2,087 runs for the Tigers from 1905-26.)

39) C – Jason Johnson (Johnson hit his home run off of former Tiger Jeff Weaver at Los Angeles in 2005.)

40) C – 2005 (Craig Monroe led the Tigers with a .277 batting average.)

41) B – Hal Newhouser (Newhouser led the AL with 25 wins, a 1.81 ERA, and 212 strikeouts in 1945.)

42) D – 24 (In 1945, the Tigers and Athletics played a 24-inning game that ended in a 1-1 tie.)

43) B – No (Leyland was signed as a catcher by Detroit in 1963 and spent six seasons in the minors before turning to coaching.)

44) C – Curtis Granderson (Granderson hit an inside-the-park home run off of Phil Hughes of the Yankees in 2007.)

45) B – 6 (Ty Cobb [.434], Johnny Bassler [.420], Hank Greenberg [.412], Harry Heilmann [.410], Charlie Gehringer [.404], and Lu Blue [.403])

46) C – Orange

47) B – Larry Parrish (2003-06 and 2008-present [Parrish missed the 2007 season due to an ankle injury.])

48) A – 1 (Al Kaline won the award in 1973. It is given to those who exemplify sportsmanship and make positive contributions to their community.)

49) A – True (The Tigers hit .261 versus RHP and .259 versus LHP.)

50) D – Bill Freehan (Freehan was hit by pitch 114 times as a Tiger [1961-76].)

Note: All answers valid as of the end of the 2009 season, unless otherwise indicated in the question itself.

1) Who is the only Tigers manager inducted into the National Baseball Hall of Fame?

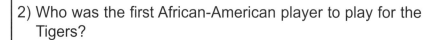

Answers begin on page 75

    A)   Sparky Anderson
    B)   Ty Cobb
    C)   Bucky Harris
    D)   Hughie Jennings

2) Who was the first African-American player to play for the Tigers?

    A)   Larry Doby
    B)   Gates Brown
    C)   Willie Horton
    D)   Earl Wilson

3) The Tigers cancelled spring training from 1943-45 due to wartime travel restrictions.

    A)   True
    B)   False

4) Where is the Tigers' Latin American Baseball Team located?

    A)   Mexico
    B)   Venezuela
    C)   Dominican Republic
    D)   Panama

5) Detroit was the first-ever team in MLB to have an African-American pitch in a game.

    A) True
    B) False

6) Who was the most recent Tiger to lead the American League in runs scored?

    A) Lou Whitaker
    B) Bobby Higginson
    C) Curtis Granderson
    D) Tony Phillips

7) What is the Tigers' record for most consecutive winning seasons?

    A) 6
    B) 8
    C) 11
    D) 13

8) How many teams has Detroit played greater than 2,000 times in the regular season?

    A) 1
    B) 3
    C) 5
    D) 7

9) Which Tiger was named MVP of the 1984 World Series?

    A) Jack Morris
    B) Larry Herndon
    C) Alan Trammell
    D) Kirk Gibson

10) Which Tigers player won the most Gold Glove Awards?

    A) Al Kaline
    B) Alan Trammell
    C) Bill Freehan
    D) Mickey Stanley

11) What team did Sparky Anderson manage before managing the Tigers?

    A) Pittsburgh Pirates
    B) Oakland A's
    C) Baltimore Orioles
    D) Cincinnati Reds

12) Curtis Granderson led the American League in triples in 2009.

    A) True
    B) False

13) Which Tigers pitcher was nicknamed "The Yankee Killer"?

A) Tommy Bridges
B) Hooks Dauss
C) Jim Bunning
D) Frank Lary

14) Which Tiger is the youngest player in MLB history to win a batting title?

A) Al Kaline
B) Harvey Kuenn
C) George Kell
D) Ty Cobb

15) Which National League team has Detroit played the greatest number of times?

A) Atlanta Braves
B) Chicago Cubs
C) Milwaukee Brewers
D) Cincinnati Reds

16) Which Tiger had the first-ever RBI at Comerica Park?

A) Dean Palmer
B) Gregg Jefferies
C) Juan Gonzalez
D) Juan Encarnacion

17) How many Tigers batters won the American League Triple Crown?

    A) 1
    B) 2
    C) 3
    D) 4

18) When was the most recent season the Tigers failed to hit 100 or more team home runs?

    A) 1981
    B) 1989
    C) 1996
    D) 2002

19) Where do the Tigers hold spring training?

    A) Phoenix, Ariz.
    B) Kissimmee, Fla.
    C) Lakeland, Fla.
    D) Scottsdale, Ariz.

20) Who is the only Tigers pitcher to lead the team in strikeouts for 10 consecutive seasons?

    A) Jim Bunning
    B) Hal Newhouser
    C) Mickey Lolich
    D) Jack Morris

21) All-time, how many managers have the Tigers had?

    A) 24
    B) 28
    C) 32
    D) 36

22) Who was the Tigers' opponent for their last game at Tiger Stadium?

    A) Cleveland Indians
    B) Kansas City Royals
    C) Toronto Blue Jays
    D) Baltimore Orioles

23) Which Tigers manager had the second highest winning percentage (minimum three seasons)?

    A) Sparky Anderson
    B) Hughie Jennings
    C) Billy Martin
    D) Mayo Smith

24) Did the Tigers have a winning record in extra-inning games in 2009?

    A) Yes
    B) No

25) What is the Tigers' record for the most times a single player has been hit by pitch in a season?

    A) 16
    B) 20
    C) 24
    D) 28

26) Which Tiger hit the last home run in Tiger Stadium?

    A) Deivi Cruz
    B) Gabe Kapler
    C) Tony Clark
    D) Robert Fick

27) What year was the Tigers' first-ever home night game in Detroit?

    A) 1945
    B) 1948
    C) 1951
    D) 1954

28) What year did a Tigers player(s) first appear on the cover of *Sports Illustrated*?

    A) 1950
    B) 1956
    C) 1962
    D) 1968

29) What decade did the Tigers have the lowest winning percentage?

    A)   1950s
    B)   1970s
    C)   1990s
    D)   2000s

30) When was the most recent season the Tigers had total home attendance of less than three million?

    A)   2000
    B)   2003
    C)   2006
    D)   2009

31) How many times have the Tigers finished in first place and failed to win the World Series?

    A)   3
    B)   5
    C)   7
    D)   9

32) What is the lowest team batting average the Tigers ever had in a single season?

    A)   .226
    B)   .231
    C)   .237
    D)   .242

33) Which pitcher holds the Tigers' career record for most strikeouts?

A) Jack Morris
B) Jim Bunning
C) Mickey Lolich
D) Hooks Dauss

34) Who is the only Tigers pitcher to win the Rolaids Relief Man Award?

A) John Hiller
B) Juan Acevedo
C) Guillermo Hernandez
D) Todd Jones

35) How many Tigers have been named American League Rookie of the Year?

A) 2
B) 4
C) 6
D) 8

36) How many times has Detroit lost in the American League Divisional Series?

A) 0
B) 1
C) 2
D) 3

37) How many times have the Tigers swept the opposing team in the World Series?

    A)   0
    B)   1
    C)   2
    D)   3

38) What was the lowest regular-season winning percentage of a Tigers World Series Championship team?

    A)   .575
    B)   .590
    C)   .607
    D)   .619

39) What is the Tigers' record for lowest team ERA in a season?

    A)   1.91
    B)   2.13
    C)   2.26
    D)   2.42

40) Have the Tigers ever had 20 or more hits in a nine-inning game they lost?

    A)   Yes
    B)   No

41) What is the nickname of the single A Tiger affiliate located in Lakeland, Fla.?

   A) Whitecaps
   B) SeaWolves
   C) Mud Hens
   D) Flying Tigers

42) Who was the most recent Tiger to win the American League batting title?

   A) Lou Whitaker
   B) Magglio Ordonez
   C) Norm Cash
   D) Ivan Rodriguez

43) How many seasons was Ernie Harwell known as "the voice of the Tigers"?

   A) 34
   B) 38
   C) 42
   D) 46

44) What was the highest winning percentage of a Tigers manager who lasted one season or less?

   A) .500
   B) .618
   C) .774
   D) 1.000

45) When was the most recent season the Tigers failed to score 600 runs?

   A) 1997
   B) 2000
   C) 2003
   D) 2006

46) Who was the most recent Tiger to lead the American League in RBIs?

   A) Cecil Fielder
   B) Miguel Cabrera
   C) Tony Clark
   D) Magglio Ordonez

47) How many total all-time no-hitters have been thrown by Tigers pitchers (includes perfect games)?

   A) 4
   B) 6
   C) 8
   D) 10

48) Who led the Tigers in slugging percentage in 2009?

   A) Curtis Granderson
   B) Brandon Inge
   C) Miguel Cabrera
   D) Magglio Ordonez

49) Which Tigers player was selected to the most career All-Star Games?

    A)   Hal Newhouser
    B)   Al Kaline
    C)   Lou Whitaker
    D)   Hank Greenberg

50) Denny McLain was the first player in MLB history to win the Cy Young Award and American League MVP in the same season.

    A)   True
    B)   False

When you think of great double-play combinations in MLB history, the Tigers' Alan Trammell and Lou Whitaker have to be right near the top of the list. The duo played together from the late 1970s through 1995, helping to lead the Tigers to 15 winning seasons and a World Series title. Their long list of achievements includes a combined eleven All-Star Game appearances, eight Silver Slugger Awards, and seven Gold Glove Awards. Throw in Whitaker's 1978 Rookie of the Year Award and Trammell's 1984 World Series MVP Trophy and the pair has won just about every major MLB award. In addition, they set the American League record for games played as teammates. Trammell and Whitaker appeared in 1,918 games together, breaking the old American League mark of 1,914 held by the Royals' George Brett and Frank White.

1) D – Hughie Jennings (Jennings managed the Tigers from 1907-20, and was inducted into the Hall of Fame in 1945.)

2) A – Larry Doby (Doby made his debut for the Tigers in 1959. Dominican-born Ozzie Virgil was the first player of color for the Tigers a few years earlier.)

3) B – False (The Tigers decided to move Spring Training from Lakeland, Fla. to Evansville, Ind.)

4) C – Dominican Republic (The Tigers Latin Baseball Academy is located in San Cristobal, Dominican Republic.)

5) B – False (The Dodgers Dan Bankhead debuted as the first African-American pitcher in MLB in 1947. The Tigers did not have an African-American pitcher until the 1960s.)

6) D – Tony Phillips (Phillips led the AL with 114 runs scored in 1992.)

7) C – 11 (The Tigers posted eight consecutive winning seasons from 1978-88.)

8) B – 3 (Cleveland Indians [2,067], Minnesota Twins [2,007], Chicago White Sox [2,002])

9) C – Alan Trammell (Trammell was named MVP after hitting .450 with 2 HRs and 6 RBIs.)

10) A – Al Kaline (Outfielder Al Kaline won 10 Gold Glove Awards for the Tigers [1957-59 and 1961-67].)

11) D – Cincinnati Reds (Anderson managed the Reds from 1970-78, leading Cincinnati to back-to-back World Series titles in 1975-76.)

12) B – False (Granderson had just 8 triples in 2009, which was tied for fifth in the AL. He led the AL in 2007 [23] and 2008 [13].)

13) D – Frank Lary (Lary pitched for the Tigers from 1954-64 and had a career record of 28-13 versus the Yankees. During the 1958-59 seasons, Lary won 13 of 14 decisions versus New York.)

14) A – Al Kaline (In 1955, 20-year-old Al Kaline led the AL in batting average [.340], becoming the youngest player in MLB history to win a batting title.)

15) C – Milwaukee Brewers (The Tigers are 221-197 all-time versus the Brewers, including a three-game sweep in 2009. The Brewers were a member of the AL from 1969-97.)

16) B – Gregg Jefferies (Jefferies' single scored Luis Polonia in the bottom of the first inning of the first-ever game at Comerica Park.)

17) A – 1 (Ty Cobb won the AL Triple Crown in 1909 with a .377 batting average, 9 home runs, and 107 RBIs.)

18) A – 1981 (The Tigers hit just 65 home runs during the strike-shortened 1981 season.)

19) C – Lakeland, Fla. (2010 will mark Detroit's 74th season holding spring training in Lakeland, Fla., the longest relationship between a team and a city in MLB.)

20) D – Jack Morris (Morris led the Tigers in strikeouts each season from 1979-88.)

21) D – 36 (Jim Leyland became Detroit's 36th all-time manager in 2006.)

22) B – Kansas City Royals (The Tigers beat the Royals 8-2. Al Kaline [Tigers] and George Brett [Royals] were honorary captains for the game.)

23) D – Mayo Smith (Smith posted a 363-285 record [.560] from 1967-70.)

24) A – Yes (The Tigers were 6-5 in extra-inning games in 2009.)

25) C – 24 (Detroit's Bill Freehan was hit by pitch 24 times during the 1968 season.)

26) D – Robert Fick (Fick hit the last home run in Tiger Stadium, a grand slam off of Kansas City's Jeff Montgomery.)

27) B – 1948 (The Tigers defeated the Philadelphia Athletics 4-1.)

28) B – 1956 (Al Kaline and Harvey Kuenn were featured on the May 14 issue.)

29) D – 2000s (The Tigers were 729-891 during the 2000s, for a .450 winning percentage.)

30) D – 2009 (Despite being in first place most of the season, the Tigers drew just 2,567,193.)

31) C – 7 (The Tigers finished in first place seven times failing to win the World Series [1907-09, 1934, 1940, 1972, and 1987].)

32) B – .231 (The Tigers hit just .231 during the 1904 season.)

33) C – Mickey Lolich (Lolich struck out 2,679 batters as a Tiger from 1963-75.)

34) D – Todd Jones (Jones won the award in 2000 after posting 42 saves.)

35) B – 4 (Harvey Kuenn [1953], Mark Fidrych [1976], Lou Whitaker [1978], and Justin Verlander [2006])

36) A – 0 (Detroit's only appearance in the ALDS came in 2006, a 3-1 series victory over the Yankees.)

37) A – 0 (The Tigers have never swept a World Series.)

38) A – .575 (The Tigers finished the 1935 regular season with an 88-65 record.)

39) C – 2.26 (The Tigers posted a 2.26 ERA during the 1909 season.)

40) A – Yes (The Tigers had 21 hits versus the White Sox in 2006, but lost the game 9-13.)

41) D – Flying Tigers (The Lakeland Flying Tigers have been the Tigers High-A affiliate since 1967.)

42) B – Magglio Ordonez (Ordonez led the AL with a .368 batting average in 2007.)

43) C – 42 (Harwell did play-by-play for the Tigers from 1960-91 and 1993-02.)

44) D – 1.000 (Two managers had this winning percentage, Billy Hitchcock [1960] and Dick Tracewski [1979].)

45) C – 2003 (The Tigers scored just 591 runs during the 2003 season.)

46) A – Cecil Fielder (Fielder led the AL with 124 RBIs in 1992.)

47) B – 6 (The last Detroit no-hitter was thrown by Justin Verlander versus Milwaukee in 2007.)

48) C – Miguel Cabrera (He led the team with a .547 slugging percentage.)

49) B – Al Kaline (Kaline was selected to 18 All-Star Games during his Tigers career.)

50) A – True (McLain became the first player to win the Cy Young Award and the AL MVP in the same season in 1968.)

Note: All answers valid as of the end of the 2009 season, unless otherwise indicated in the question itself.

1) How many Tigers managers have won at least one World Series?

Answers begin on page 83

    A) 1
    B) 2
    C) 3
    D) 4

2) All-time, how many World Series games have the Tigers lost by a single run?

    A) 4
    B) 8
    C) 12
    D) 16

3) How many overall No. 1 draft picks have the Tigers had?

    A) 0
    B) 1
    C) 2
    D) 3

4) Did Sparky Anderson win his last-ever game as a Tigers manager?

    A) Yes
    B) No

5) What are the most wins by a Tigers pitcher in a single season?

    A) 23
    B) 27
    C) 31
    D) 35

6) Who holds the Tigers' record for most doubles in a season?

    A) Ty Cobb
    B) Gee Walker
    C) Dmitri Young
    D) Hank Greenberg

7) How many times has Detroit finished the regular season in first place?

    A) 8
    B) 11
    C) 14
    D) 17

8) Detroit has more outfielders than pitchers enshrined in the National Baseball Hall of Fame.

    A) True
    B) False

9) Which Tigers relief pitcher made the most appearances in 2009?

    A)   Bobby Seay
    B)   Ryan Perry
    C)   Brandon Lyon
    D)   Fernando Rodney

10) What is the Tigers' record for most runs scored in a nine-inning game?

    A)   18
    B)   21
    C)   24
    D)   27

Tigerology Trivia Challenge

1) D – 4 (Mickey Cochrane [1935], Steve O'Neill [1945], Mayo Smith [1968], and Sparky Anderson [1984])

2) A – 4 (The Tigers have lost 33 all-time World Series games, four of them by a single run.)

3) B – 1 (The Tigers selected pitcher Matt Anderson from Rice University with the first overall pick in 1997.)

4) B – No (The Tigers lost 0-4 at Baltimore in 1995.)

5) C – 31 (Denny McLain won 31 games for the Tigers in 1968 and is the most recent pitcher in MLB to win 30 games in a season.)

6) D – Hank Greenberg (Greenberg hit 63 doubles in 1934.)

7) B – 11 (1907, 1908, 1909, 1934, 1935, 1940, 1945, 1968, 1972, 1984, and 1987)

8) A – True (The Tigers have five outfielders enshrined [Ty Cobb, Sam Crawford, Harry Heilmann, Al Kaline, and Heinie Manush] and just one pitcher [Hal Newhouser].)

9) D – Fernando Rodney (Rodney appeared in 73 games in 2009.)

10) B – 21 (4 times [most recently at Chicago White Sox in 1936])

Note: All answers valid as of the end of the 2009 season, unless otherwise indicated in the question itself.

Player / Team Score Sheet

Name:_____

Spring Training		Regular Season		Postseason		Championship Series		Extra Innings Bonus	
1	26	1	26	1	26	1	26	1	
2	27	2	27	2	27	2	27	2	
3	28	3	28	3	28	3	28	3	
4	29	4	29	4	29	4	29	4	
5	30	5	30	5	30	5	30	5	
6	31	6	31	6	31	6	31	6	
7	32	7	32	7	32	7	32	7	
8	33	8	33	8	33	8	33	8	
9	34	9	34	9	34	9	34	9	
10	35	10	35	10	35	10	35	10	
11	36	11	36	11	36	11	36		
12	37	12	37	12	37	12	37		
13	38	13	38	13	38	13	38		
14	39	14	39	14	39	14	39		
15	40	15	40	15	40	15	40		
16	41	16	41	16	41	16	41		
17	42	17	42	17	42	17	42		
18	43	18	43	18	43	18	43		
19	44	19	44	19	44	19	44		
20	45	20	45	20	45	20	45		
21	46	21	46	21	46	21	46		
22	47	22	47	22	47	22	47		
23	48	23	48	23	48	23	48		
24	49	24	49	24	49	24	49		
25	50	25	50	25	50	25	50		
___ x 1 = ___		___ x 2 = ___		___ x 3 = ___		___ x 4 = ___		___ x 4 = ___	

Multiply total number correct by point value/quarter to calculate totals for each quarter.

Add total of all quarters below.

Total Points:_____

Thank you for playing *Tigerology Trivia Challenge*.

Additional score sheets are available at:
www.TriviaGameBooks.com

Player / Team Score Sheet

Name:_____

Spring Training			Regular Season			Postseason			Championship Series			Extra Innings Bonus	
1		26	1		26	1		26	1		26	1	
2		27	2		27	2		27	2		27	2	
3		28	3		28	3		28	3		28	3	
4		29	4		29	4		29	4		29	4	
5		30	5		30	5		30	5		30	5	
6		31	6		31	6		31	6		31	6	
7		32	7		32	7		32	7		32	7	
8		33	8		33	8		33	8		33	8	
9		34	9		34	9		34	9		34	9	
10		35	10		35	10		35	10		35	10	
11		36	11		36	11		36	11		36		
12		37	12		37	12		37	12		37		
13		38	13		38	13		38	13		38		
14		39	14		39	14		39	14		39		
15		40	15		40	15		40	15		40		
16		41	16		41	16		41	16		41		
17		42	17		42	17		42	17		42		
18		43	18		43	18		43	18		43		
19		44	19		44	19		44	19		44		
20		45	20		45	20		45	20		45		
21		46	21		46	21		46	21		46		
22		47	22		47	22		47	22		47		
23		48	23		48	23		48	23		48		
24		49	24		49	24		49	24		49		
25		50	25		50	25		50	25		50		

____x 1 =____   ____x 2 =____   ____x 3 =____   ____x 4 =____   ____x 4 =____

Multiply total number correct by point value/quarter to calculate totals for each quarter.

Add total of all quarters below.

Total Points:_____

Thank you for playing *Tigerology Trivia Challenge*.

**Additional score sheets are available at:
www.TriviaGameBooks.com**